Gila Monsters

By JoAnn Early Macken

Reading Consultant: Jeanne Clidas, Ph.D.
Director, Roberts Wesleyan College Literacy Clinic

WEEKLY READER®
PUBLISHING

Please visit our web site at **www.garethstevens.com**.
For a free catalog describing our list of high-quality books,
call 1-877-542-2595 (USA) or 1-800-387-3178 (Canada).
Our fax: 1-877-542-2596

Library of Congress Cataloging-in-Publication Data

Macken, JoAnn Early, 1953–
    Gila monsters / by JoAnn Early Macken; reading consultant, Jeanne Clidas.
        p. cm. — (Animals that live in the desert)
    Includes bibliographical references and index.
    ISBN-10: 1-4339-1951-6   ISBN-13: 978-1-4339-1951-0 (lib. bdg.)
    ISBN-10: 1-4339-2449-8   ISBN-13: 978-1-4339-2449-1 (soft cover)
    1. Lizards—Juvenile literature. I. Title.
  QL666.L2M23   2010
  597.95'952—dc22   2009002863

This edition first published in 2010 by
Weekly Reader® Books
An Imprint of Gareth Stevens Publishing
1 Reader's Digest Road
Pleasantville, NY 10570-7000 USA

Executive Managing Editor: Lisa M. Herrington
Senior Editor: Barbara Bakowski
Project Management: Spooky Cheetah Press
Cover Designers: Jennifer Ryder-Talbot and Studio Montage
Production: Studio Montage
Library Consultant: Carl Harvey, Library Media Specialist, Noblesville, Indiana

Photo credits: Cover, p. 17 Shutterstock; pp. 1, 13 © Lynn M. Stone; pp. 5, 9, 21 © John Cancalosi/
naturepl.com; p. 7 © Jeff Foott/naturepl.com; p. 11 © Joe McDonald/Visuals Unlimited;
pp. 15, 19 © Jim Merli/Visuals Unlimited

Printed in the United States of America

1 2 3 4 5 6 7 8 9 14 13 12 11 10 09

Table of Contents

Boldface words appear in the glossary.

Giant Lizard

The Gila (HEEL-ah) monster is a lizard. It is the largest lizard that lives in the United States. Its bite has poison called **venom**.

Lizards are **reptiles**. They move into the sun to warm up. They hide in the shade to stay cool.

091873

7

Gila monsters live in the **desert**. They hide most of the time. In the summer, they rest under the ground. In the winter, they **hibernate**, or sleep.

The Gila monster is covered with **scales**. The scales look like beads. Some scales are black. Some are pink or orange.

scales

11

The Gila monster has strong claws. Its tongue is purple. The tip is forked, or split into two points.

claws

tongue

Meals for a Monster

Gila monsters have sharp teeth. They eat eggs from birds, snakes, and turtles. They also eat small animals.

A Gila monster can eat a huge meal. It may not eat again for a long time. It stores fat in its tail. Later, it lives on the fat.

tail

Strong From the Start

Female Gila monsters lay eggs in the sand. The eggs stay warm in the sun. Babies **hatch** from the eggs. The babies have teeth and venom.

babies

eggs

19

If a Gila monster is scared, it tries to back away. It may even open its mouth and hiss. If it cannot escape, it may bite!

Fast Facts

Length	about 2 feet (61 centimeters) nose to tail
Weight	about 4 pounds (2 kilograms)
Diet	small animals, frogs, birds, and eggs
Average life span	up to 30 years

Glossary

desert: a dry area with little rainfall

hatch: to come out of an egg

hibernate: to go into a deep sleep for a long time

reptiles: animals that breathe air, have a backbone, and usually have scales or bony plates on their bodies, such as alligators, lizards, snakes, or turtles

scales: thin, flat plates that cover the bodies of snakes, fish, and other animals

venom: poison

For More Information

Books

Gila Monsters. Early Bird Nature Books (series).
Conrad J. Storad (Lerner, 2007)

Gila Monsters. World of Reptiles (series).
Jason Glaser (Capstone Press, 2006)

Web Sites

Gila Monster

*animals.nationalgeographic.com/animals/reptiles/
gila-monster.html*
Watch a short video about a Gila monster.

Gila Monster

www.whozoo.org/anlife2000/jamiebritt/gilaindexrev.html
Read all about the Gila monster. See cool photos, too.

Publisher's note to educators and parents: Our editors have carefully reviewed these web sites to ensure that they are suitable for children. Many web sites change frequently, however, and we cannot guarantee that a site's future contents will continue to meet our high standards of quality and educational value. Be advised that children should be closely supervised whenever they access the Internet.

Index

About the Author

JoAnn Early Macken is the author of two rhyming picture books, *Sing-Along Song* and *Cats on Judy*, and more than 80 nonfiction books for children. Her poems have appeared in several children's magazines. She lives in Wisconsin with her husband and their two sons.